For Thea and Max
with *oceans* of love

In memory of
Mrs. Huntoon and,
of course, Nani

Library of Congress Cataloging-in-Publication Data
Berger, Carin.
Not so true stories and unreasonable rhymes / by Carin Berger.
p. cm.
ISBN 0-8118-3773-4
1.Children's poetry, American. 2. Nonsense verses, American.
I.Title.
PS3602.E7534N68 2004
811'.6–dc21
2003003666

Book design by Carin Berger
and Sara Gillingham.
Typeset in Bernhard Modern.
The illustrations in this book were
rendered in cut-paper collage.
Manufactured in China.

Distributed in Canada by Raincoast Books
9050 Shaughnessy Street, Vancouver, British Columbia V6P 6E5

10 9 8 7 6 5 4 3 2

Chronicle Books LLC
85 Second Street, San Francisco, California 94105

www.chroniclekids.com

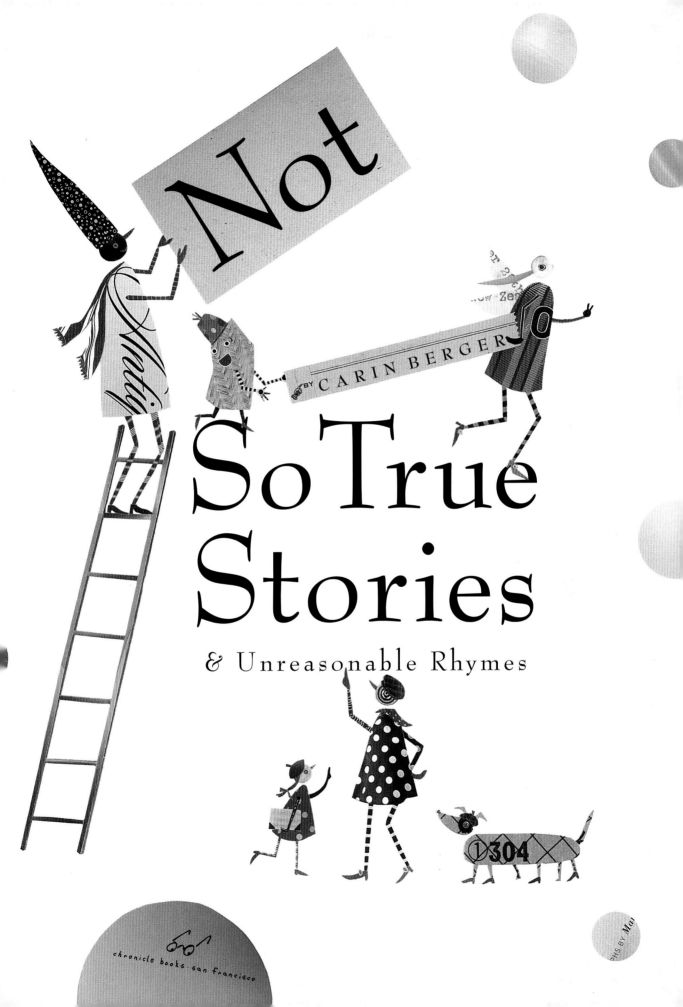

# Not

## So True Stories

### & Unreasonable Rhymes

BY CARIN BERGER

chronicle books · san francisco

# Galaxy Race

Ready! Set!
It's the Galaxy Race
With sparky flies *whizzing*
Through deep outer space
They go and go and go

*Zooming*

Flashy bright red cars

They *madly dash* from star to star

Instead of maps they use radar

Which glow and glow and glow

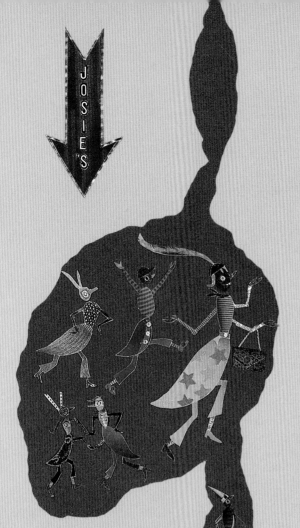

# Josie's Cabaret

One hundred ants
In lime green pants
　　Are feeling so *très, très*

Beetle bugs
With scarlet gloves
　　*Shimmy,* b o p and *s w a y*

Swooping bats
In silk top hats
　　And nimble spider acrobats

All swing to Ella, Duke and Fats

At **Josie's Cabaret**

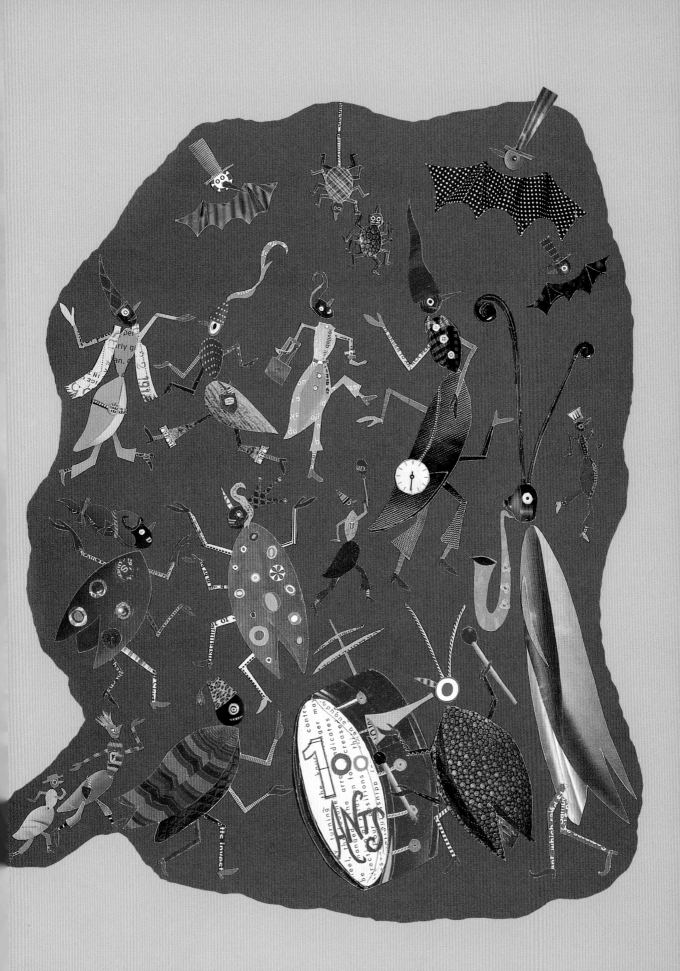

# SneaKer SnaKes

Slippery, slidey
Sneak-around snakes
Wish they had sneakers
But make no mistake
With *swirly* green eyes

And slithery tongues

It's a very good thing
They can't lace up and *r u n*

# Mr. Mean

Lean little Mr. Mean

Eats a **sour** tangerine

He *squishes* up his pucker lips

So Cheery Cherry

Gives a KisS

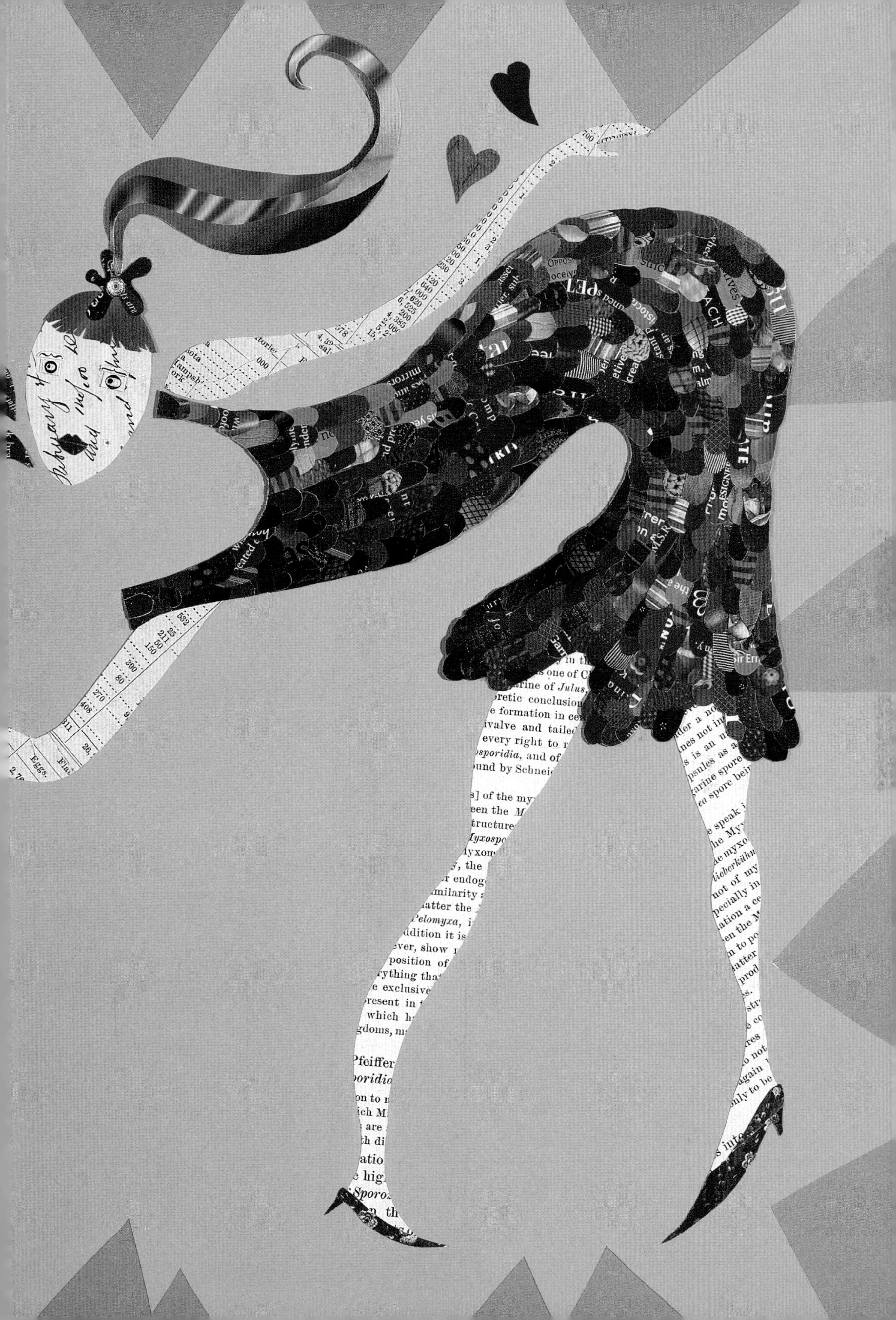

# Train

Hey, Mr. Subway Train
Won't you take me
for a ride

With all those riders
side by side
Whooshing
through a tunnel

Other trains flash past my eyes
Fast and f a s t e r
we all fly

While I sit still
the world **streaks** by
What a lot of
f u n – n e l

# Zeppelins

One thousand shiny zeppelins
Soar through midnight skies
Flown by spotted ladybugs
And errant dragonflies

They dip and glide past rosy clouds
And glowing silver moons
While shadows dance and crickets sing
They land on nightshade blooms

# Rodeo Rosy

Rough Riding Rosy the rodeo star

Rides romping red rhinos but *never* gets far

Those rhinos REFUSE and trod on her boots

So Rough Riding Rosy is getting a *car*

# Beach Song

Lavender hills, indigo sea

Lemon-drop sun shines down with glee

Aqua green waves crash and subside

Sandy brown beaches and marshmallow tides

# Very Best of Friends

Wiley Croc and Goldie Fish were very best of friends

Until the sad and bitter day with which this story ends

While swimming s l o w l y in the swamp

Old Wiley gave a y a w n

He sucked poor Goldie in his mouth and

## GULP!

His friend was gone

# Flock O' Birdies

Birdy **1** and Birdy **2**
Dance a *groovy boogaloo*

Birdy **3** and Birdy **4**
Fluff each other's
Pompadours

Birdy **5** and Birdy **6**
(whose names are Clive and Mr. Fix)
know **many**
marvelous magic tricks

Birdy **7** and Birdy **8**
Are *always* early,
*never* late

Birdy **9** and Birdy 10
*Zoom* to the moon
(and back again)

# Lovely Lucy

Lovely Lucy Lemonhead

Is **sour** as can be

She needs three scoops of jelly jam

Between each sip of tea

She goes through sweetie biscuits

At a most ALARMING pace

But still she is a **sourpuss**

A frown upon her face

Daddy-O

I call my daddy Daddy-O, cuz he's the coolest cat I know.  He's a

jumping jiving

HiP fellow, my funKy, hunky Daddy-O

# FOxY FoX

Fox is out tonight

Fox is out tonight

He's running 'round all over town

And dancing to the *jazzy* sounds

He's **dressing up** and **boogying down**

At all the finest places

Foxy Fox is *super fine*

Out celebrating all the time

In sly red boots, plaid pants divine

He's gone by dawn without a sign

The Fox, he leaves no t r a c e s

# Rock-a-Bye

Rock-a-bye, rock-a-bye, lollipop moon

The sun's gone away and none too soon

For dreamy-time flowers are waiting to bloom

So come to me, come to me

Lullaby moon